MLB HOT STREAKS

BY EMMA HUDDLESTON

MOMENTUM

The Child's World®
childsworld.com

Published by The Child's World®
1980 Lookout Drive • Mankato, MN 56003-1705
800-599-READ • www.childsworld.com

ISBN 9781503832299
LCCN 2018962885

Printed in the United States of America
PA02422

ABOUT THE AUTHOR

Emma Huddleston lives in Minnesota with her husband. She enjoys writing
children's books, but she likes reading novels even more. When she is not writing
or reading, she likes to stay active by running, hiking, or swing dancing.

CONTENTS

MOMENTUM

FAST FACTS

Basic Information

► Each baseball game has nine **innings**, and each team has nine players on the field. There are two halves to each inning. In the top half, one team pitches while the other hits. Then they switch for the bottom half.

► The team up to bat wants to score **runs**. To score, a hitter must run around all three bases and back to home plate. When batters get three **strikes**, they are out. Three outs means the teams change from batting to fielding.

► The team in the field wants to get three outs as fast as possible. Some of the ways they can get an out include catching the ball before it hits the ground or tagging opposing players as they run the bases.

Major League Baseball Is Born

► Major League Baseball (MLB) began in 1903. It has two leagues: the American League and the National League. Today there are 30 MLB teams, and 15 play in each league.

► The World Series determines the MLB champion each fall.

**In 2018, the Boston Red Sox beat the Los Angeles ►
Dodgers to win the World Series.**

CHAPTER ONE

DIMAGGIO'S 56-GAME HITTING STREAK

Joe DiMaggio tightened his grip around the bat. It was the bottom of the first inning, and his New York Yankees were facing the Chicago White Sox. His eyes were on the pitcher. DiMaggio saw the pitcher swing his leg, so he got ready to hit the ball. DiMaggio could feel the ball hit his bat. He watched it fly into the field. DiMaggio reached first base, and his hit allowed his teammate to score. This is called a **run batted in (RBI)**. He smiled and shook hands with his teammates after the inning. DiMaggio did not realize what he had started.

In the 1941 season, DiMaggio went on a hitting hot streak. Game after game, he got at least one hit. After 30 **consecutive** games, his streak was still alive. But when the Yankees played the St. Louis Browns, DiMaggio's streak almost ended at 35 games.

◄ **Joe DiMaggio takes a swing while at bat during a 1941 game.**

▲ **DiMaggio's hitting streak started on May 15, 1941. It ended on July 17.**

It was the bottom on the eighth inning, and DiMaggio had not gotten a hit yet. He was sitting on the bench. He looked out at the pitcher. He watched the pitcher's motion on the mound. DiMaggio knew he could get a hit. In the eighth inning, DiMaggio got his chance. He had his eyes locked on the pitcher. He was focused.

When the ball got close enough, DiMaggio swung and smacked it for a hit. His hot streak continued, and the Yankees won the game 9–1.

On July 2, 1941, the Yankees played the Boston Red Sox. DiMaggio's hitting streak had been going on for more than one month. He was almost up to bat and was ready to go. DiMaggio stepped up to the plate. When he hit the ball, it flew into the outfield and over the fence. DiMaggio had hit a home run. The crowd cheered as he rounded the bases.

DiMaggio's hitting continued his streak. The major league record was 44, but he didn't stop there. DiMaggio got a hit in 56 consecutive games. His impressive streak ended when the Yankees played the Cleveland Indians and DiMaggio did not get a hit. However, his hot streak was an MLB all-time record.

DIMAGGIO AND HEINZ

Everyone took notice of DiMaggio's hot streak. The Heinz ketchup company hoped he would make it to 57 games—that would match the number on their ketchup labels. The company promised to give him $10,000 if he did. However, DiMaggio's hot streak ended at game 56, so he did not get the money.

▲ **Hershiser has said that his confidence grew during his hot streak.**

As the game went on, he threw more than a scoreless inning. He threw a **shutout**. The Braves didn't score at all, and the Dodgers won 3–0.

A few days later, Hershiser was nervous. The Dodgers hosted the Cincinnati Reds. Hershiser knew every pitch mattered. He straightened his hat and looked at the batter. Then he swung his leg up and forcefully threw the ball. It made a thumping noise when it hit the catcher's glove. Hershiser continued to concentrate on each pitch. The Dodgers finally came through with five runs to win it. Hershiser had pitched another shutout.

◄ **Hershiser celebrates the end of an inning in 1988.**

His streak continued. Hershiser threw three more shutouts and had put together nearly 50 consecutive scoreless innings in all. Then the Dodgers went to San Diego, California, to play the Padres.

Sweat dripped down Hershiser's face as he pitched. The game was close. Hershiser threw one scoreless inning. Then he threw another. The MLB record was 58 straight scoreless innings. Hershiser tied the record in the ninth inning. But neither team had scored, so the game went on. He knew he needed to finish this inning without letting the other team score.

There were two outs, and he was ready to pitch. He took a deep breath and prepared himself. He focused on the batter.

MOST VALUABLE PLAYER

Hershiser's streak was still going when the season ended. Playoffs don't count toward records. But unofficially Hershiser's streak continued in the National League Championship Series. The Dodgers played the New York Mets. Hershiser pitched eight more scoreless innings. That meant his streak reached 67 consecutive scoreless innings. He was later named the Most Valuable Player of both this series and the World Series.

▲ The Dodgers went on to win the 1988 World Series. Hershiser's teammates lifted him into the air after the win.

The ball zoomed toward home plate, and the batter swung his bat. The ball flew into the outfield. As soon as his teammate caught the ball, Hershiser smiled. He had the MLB record for most scoreless innings in a row with 59. Hershiser said, "We just had a really good team, it wasn't about me, I was always just part of the whole."[1] However, Hershiser's hot streak ended when he gave up a run in the first inning of the following season.

CHAPTER THREE

WOOD'S 20 STRIKEOUTS

Kerry Wood made May 6, 1998, a memorable day in MLB history. Some people call it the greatest-pitched game of all time. As the game was about to start, Wood pulled his Chicago Cubs hat down on his head. The Houston Astros were one of the best teams in the league, and he knew he needed to pitch well against them. When he faced the first Astros batter, he used the catcher's glove as a target. He aimed and threw the ball hard. He got a **strikeout** against the first batter.

Then, Wood kept throwing strikes, and the Astros could not keep up. Wood was on a hot streak. The crowd couldn't believe it when he struck out five players in a row. Wood felt confident and in control of each pitch. He didn't even realize he was getting close to breaking a record because he was focused on winning the game.

◀ **Kerry Wood was a rookie with the Chicago Cubs when he pitched in the May 6 game.**

▲ **Wood's teammates congratulate him on a great game.**

In the eighth inning, the Cubs were winning only 1–0. Wood wanted to avoid letting the Astros get a run. He gripped the ball again. He could feel the seams of the baseball under his fingers. He looked toward home plate and got ready to pitch. He threw it hard and put some spin behind the ball. The batter missed and gave Wood his 16th strikeout. Wood noticed the Cubs fans cheering loudly in the stands.

▲ **The Cubs celebrate their 1998 victory over the Astros.**

Everyone had their eyes on Wood in the last inning. He had just broken the National League record for most strikeouts in one game. If he struck out one more player, he would tie the MLB record. Wood pitched the ball as hard as he could. It curved away from the batter, who swung and missed. The crowd erupted into cheers. Wood punched his fist in celebration. He had tied the MLB record with 20 strikeouts in one game. On top of that, the Astros only got one hit the whole game. Looking back on the game, Wood said, "It definitely was a defining moment. . . . It set the bar for the rest of my career."[2]

CHAPTER FOUR

PUJOLS'S RED-HOT HITTING

It was Game 3 of the 2011 World Series when Albert Pujols and the St. Louis Cardinals were playing the Texas Rangers. Pujols stepped up to the plate and raised his bat. He watched the pitcher get ready to throw the ball. Pujols saw the ball approaching him, so he swung and hit the ball hard. It flew through the air and into the stands. Pujols hit a home run and began a dominant run of success.

In the seventh inning the Cardinals led 12–6. Pujols squirted some water into his mouth. Then, it was his turn to bat. When he got up to the plate, he gripped the bat tightly. He made contact with the ball again. It flew through the air and did not stop until it was in the crowd. Pujols had hit another home run. As he ran the bases, the crowd cheered. When he got to home plate, he gave his teammate a double high five.

◄ **Albert Pujols watches as the ball soars through the air and over the fence for a home run.**

▲ **Pujols and the Cardinals got hot against Texas in the World Series.**

The game lasted four hours. In the last inning, Pujols was tired, but he didn't show it. He looked out at the pitcher. When the ball started coming toward him, he waited to get the timing just right. He swung and felt the bat whack the ball. It soared through the air and past the wall. Pujols had hit three home runs in one game. He ran around the bases while the Cardinals fans in the crowd stood and clapped. His teammates on the bench were also cheering. They surrounded Pujols and gave him hugs. Some also patted him on the back and on the helmet.

The Cardinals won 16–7, and Pujols had dominated the game. He had three home runs, five hits, six RBIs, and 14 total bases.

▲ The Cardinals celebrate after winning
the 2011 World Series.

But he did not brag. He said, "Just pretty special, you know. But at the same time, you need to enjoy this for a moment and be ready to play tomorrow."[3]

It was a close competition between the Cardinals and the Rangers. The Rangers won Game 4 and Game 5, so there was pressure on the Cardinals in Game 6. The Cardinals ended up winning by one run when David Freese hit a home run in the 11th inning. Then, in Game 7, the Cardinals won and became the 2011 World Series Champions.

CHAPTER FIVE

CLEVELAND WINS 22 IN A ROW

Cleveland Indians fans were wound up during the 2017 regular season. On August 24, the Indians were beating the Boston Red Sox. Francisco Lindor stepped up to bat for the Indians. He had a tight grip on the bat, and his eyes were on the pitcher. The ball started coming toward him. It was a fastball, and Lindor was ready for it. He slammed the ball, and it soared through the air over the fence. It was a home run. The Indians beat the Red Sox 13–6. It started a winning streak that would become an MLB record.

Less than one week later, the Indians played the New York Yankees. Lindor was playing **shortstop**. The sun was beating down on his back. He bent his knees and got ready for the play. The batter hit the ball, and it was a straight shot between Lindor and his teammate. Lindor had to react fast. He dove to his right.

◄ **Francisco Lindor (left) is congratulated by a teammate after hitting a home run against the Red Sox.**

His whole body hit the dirt as he snatched the ball off the ground. He quickly got up and threw the ball to first base. It was an out. Lindor's quick reaction made the play. The whole team worked together throughout the game. The Indians won and continued their hot streak.

The Indians had won 21 games in a row, which set an American League record. Then they had a challenging game against Kansas City. The Indians were losing 2–1 in the bottom of the ninth. Lindor was up to bat.

He hit the ball out into left field. It flew through the air and slammed into the wall. A Kansas City player ran after it. He jumped up the wall to catch it, but the ball bounced behind him. Lindor's hit drove in a run to tie the game. The next inning, Cleveland scored one more run to win the game. The team's winning streak was now at 22.

SINGLE SEASON WINS

The 2001 Seattle Mariners team and the 1906 Chicago Cubs team both won 116 games in a single season. That is the MLB record for most victories by a team in a season.

▲ Indians' player Roberto Perez steps up to
bat against the New York Yankees.

LONGEST WINNING STREAKS FOR EACH MLB TEAM

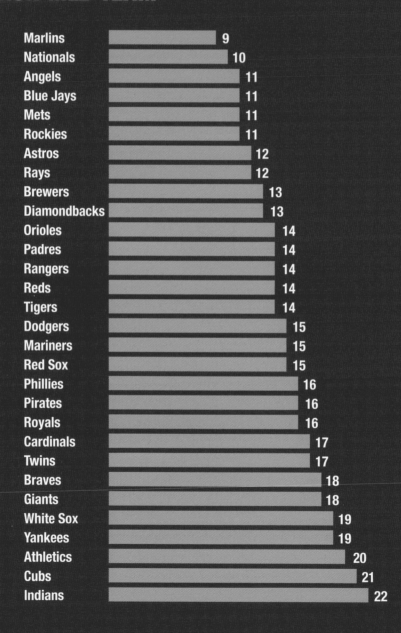

Marlins	9
Nationals	10
Angels	11
Blue Jays	11
Mets	11
Rockies	11
Astros	12
Rays	12
Brewers	13
Diamondbacks	13
Orioles	14
Padres	14
Rangers	14
Reds	14
Tigers	14
Dodgers	15
Mariners	15
Red Sox	15
Phillies	16
Pirates	16
Royals	16
Cardinals	17
Twins	17
Braves	18
Giants	18
White Sox	19
Yankees	19
Athletics	20
Cubs	21
Indians	22

However, the streak came to an end. Kansas City beat the Indians the next day. The final score was 4–3. For many people, it did not matter that the Indians lost. The fans stood and cheered to congratulate the Indians on their 22-game winning streak.

"It's pretty crazy to think about, just because you play so many games in so many days over such long stretches," said Indians' player Corey Kluber about the streak. "To go almost three weeks without losing a game is not something that you ever really expect."[4]

THINK ABOUT IT

► Do you think a person's individual hot streak can be accomplished without the help of his or her team? Explain your answer.

► Do you think practice is important if you want to do well in a sport? Why or why not?

► How do you think Wood stayed focused during his 20-strikeout game? There was a lot of pressure on him at the end of the game when he was getting close to breaking the record. What is one way an athlete can stay focused when there is a lot of pressure?

GLOSSARY

consecutive (kuhn-SEK-yuh-tiv): Consecutive means it happened in a row. DiMaggio had a hitting hot streak for 56 consecutive games.

innings (IN-ings): Innings are a part of a baseball game where each team gets a turn to bat. There are nine innings in a MLB game.

run batted in (RBI) (RUN BAT-ed IN): A run batted in (RBI) happens when the batter hits the ball so a teammate can score. DiMaggio's RBI single allowed his teammate to score.

runs (RUNZ): Runs are points in baseball. The Indians were on a winning streak because they scored more runs than the other teams.

scoreless (SKOR-less): Scoreless means the team did not get any runs. Hershiser is remembered for pitching 59 consecutive scoreless innings.

shortstop (SHORT-stop): Shortstop is a baseball position between second and third base. Lindor played shortstop.

shutout (SHUT-out): A shutout happens when one team does not let the other team score in a single game. The Dodgers beat some teams in shutout games.

strikeout (STRIKE-out): A strikeout means that a batter had three strikes, so the batter is out. Wood pitched a strikeout.

strikes (STRIKES): Strikes are pitches that are thrown so the batter can hit the ball, but the batter does not hit it. Pitchers practice throwing strikes.

SOURCE NOTES

1. Bill Plaschke. "Orel Hershiser's Streak Was a Different Ballgame." *Los Angeles Times.* Los Angeles Times, 23 July 2015. Web. 3 Jan. 2019.

2. Alyson Footer and Carrie Muskat. "Remembering the Most Dominant Start Ever." *MLB.* MLB Advanced Media, 6 May 2018. Web. 3 Jan. 2019.

3. Mark Memmott. "Pujols Has 'Greatest Night' Ever, Cards Lead World Series 2–1." *NPR.* NPR, 23 Oct. 2011. Web. 3 Jan. 2019.

4. Jordan Bastian. "'The Streak' Lives on in Indians, MLB History." *MLB.* MLB Advanced Media, 26 Dec. 2017. Web. 3 Jan. 2019.

TO LEARN MORE

BOOKS

Bryant, Howard. *Legends: The Best Players, Games, and Teams in Baseball.* New York, NY: Philomel Books, 2015.

Kelley, K. C. *Baseball Superstars 2016.* New York, NY: Scholastic, 2016.

Sports Illustrated Kids Baseball: Then to Wow!
New York, NY: Time Inc. Books, 2016.

WEBSITES

Visit our website for links about MLB: **childsworld.com/links**

Note to Parents, Teachers, and Librarians: We routinely verify our Web links to make sure they are safe and active sites. So encourage your readers to check them out!

INDEX